21st Century Skills **INNOVATION** *Library*

Music

by Annie Buckley

INNOVATION IN ENTERTAINMENT

Published in the United States of America by Cherry Lake Publishing
Ann Arbor, Michigan
www.cherrylakepublishing.com

Content Adviser: Carlos Abril, Professor of Music, Northwestern University

Design: The Design Lab

Photo Credits: Cover and page 3, ©iStockphoto.com/track5; page 4, ©iStockphoto.com/quavondo;
page 5, ©Vova Pomortzeff/Alamy; page 7, ©iStockphoto.com/Spanic; page 9, ©Melvyn
Longhurst/Alamy; page 10, ©iStockphoto.com/FotoW; page 11, ©iStockphoto.com/syagci; page
12, ©iStockphoto.com/ranplett; page 15, ©iStockphoto.com/vm; pages 16 and 25, ©iStockphoto.
com/HultonArchive; page 17, ©Gautier Willaume, used under license from Shutterstock, Inc.;
page 19, ©TerryM, used under license from Shutterstock, Inc.; page 20, ©iStockphoto.com/
MichaelDeLeon; page 22, ©iStockphoto.com/sandsun; page 23, ©iStockphoto.com/sunnyart;
page 27, ©Pictorial Press Ltd/Alamy; page 28, ©Content Mine International/Alamy

Library of Congress Cataloging-in-Publication Data
Buckley, Annie.
Music / by Annie Buckley.
   p. cm.–(Innovation in entertainment)
Includes index.
ISBN-13: 978-1-60279-220-3
ISBN-10: 1-60279-220-8
1. Music–History and criticism–Juvenile literature. I. Title. II. Series.
ML3928.B83 2009
780–dc22   2008007238

Cherry Lake Publishing would like to acknowledge the work of
The Partnership for 21st Century Skills.
Please visit www.21stcenturyskills.org for more information.

CONTENTS

CHAPTER ONE

Songs from the Past

Headphones allow you to enjoy your favorite music without disturbing others around you.

When you listen to your favorite music, you are joining a tradition that is thousands of years old! From Africa to Australia, Canada to China, Hawaii to Havana, people all over the world have made and listened to music for generations.

Archaeologists have studied objects that have been buried for **centuries**, to try to piece together what life was

The ancient Egyptians sometimes created images of musicians on the walls of their temples or tombs.

like a long time ago. For example, scientists found bones drilled with small holes. These are thought to be some of the very first instruments. Just like flutes and whistles, **ancient** people blew into these to make music. Other ancient instruments, such as rattles and drums, have been discovered around the world. Although we can imagine early people playing instruments and singing along, exactly what their music sounded like remains a mystery.

Ancient people most likely made music for many of the same reasons we do today—to dance, sing and

21st Century Content

 Different kinds of scientists and scholars help write and understand music history. Anthropologists study cultures, comparing and contrasting how people live around the world. A musicologist is a person who studies the history of music, including the performance of music and music theory (ideas about music). Like anthropologists, ethnomusicologists study humanity, but they look directly at why and how people make music. Why do you think people all over the world make music? What is special about music to you?

celebrate, or to express feelings. Music is a kind of language, but instead of words, it has **notes**, a **beat**, and a **rhythm**. One of the most exciting things about music is the way in which it opens doors between different cultures and languages. Through music, people can try to understand one another and share experiences.

The history of music covers thousands of years and spans the entire globe. Let's explore some of the major developments in music that make it such a wonderful, expressive art form enjoyed by billions of people.

CHAPTER TWO

Shake and Strum, Tap and Clap

Open your mouth and let out a sound—a nice, soft AAAAAAAA. Can you move the **pitch** up and down, higher and lower? This movement is similar to going up and down a **scale** in music. The basic elements of music are mirrored in our bodies. Place your hand on your heart and feel your pulse. Music has a similar repetitive sound, or beat that repeats, just like your heart pumps blood over and over. Our breathing also makes a pattern—in and out, in and out—like the rhythm of a song.

One of the basic steps in learning to play the piano—or any instrument—is becoming familiar with the tones of the musical scale.

The history of instruments is really a story of innovation. Each instrument has developed over time because people have used their imaginations to **adapt** the form of an instrument. People have developed instruments that sound clearer or louder or have more variety.

Remember the bone with the holes drilled in it? Ancient people drilled holes in those bones and hollowed out sticks and branches. They did this so they would be able to blow into the end of the instrument and make different sounds. This basic technology has survived thousands of years. Over time, people have stretched, decorated, updated, and transformed this instrument to develop the sound of the flute. Some adaptations have been made based on where people live. In North Africa and South America, people made whistles from dried gourds because the gourds were available to them. Native Australians invented a clever way to empty out the center of a tube to make a similar instrument. They bury a eucalyptus branch underground and let termites eat through the center. Then the people dig up the stick that has been hollowed out by the termites. They decorate it and use it to make music. This instrument is called a **didjeridoo**.

Pipes or flutes made from natural materials are still used in many parts of the world. There are also modern

The didjeridoo is an ancient instrument. People have been making didjeridoos for about 1,000 years.

counterparts made from metal, wood, or plastic. These instruments are called wind instruments, because you must blow into them to play them. Sometimes children learn to play on a basic wind instrument called a recorder. Some musicians play wind instruments such as the saxophone, trumpet, or trombone. The flute, clarinet, piccolo, and oboe are other wind instruments. All have evolved over time as musicians adapted them to make the sounds they were trying to achieve.

Many other instruments have developed over a similar history of playing, innovation, and use. String instruments require a player to pluck or strum a set of

The clarinet gets its name from the Italian word *clarinetto*, which means "little clear one."

The lute and similar instruments date back many centuries. By the 1500s, musicians could refer to instructional books and printed music made for the lute.

tightly drawn strings. The ancient Greek lyre inspired the modern-day harp, a very important instrument in classical, gypsy, and Appalachian music. Another string instrument called the lute developed in ancient China, Japan, and Africa. This instrument is closely related to the guitar, a popular instrument played all over the world today.

The piano has a history of bringing music into homes. The piano was an innovation of the 15th century. Plucking strings could be hard on fingers, so early pianos resolved this problem by attaching strings to wooden keys that were less painful to manipulate. The piano has evolved into the grand piano and the electronic keyboard.

Percussion instruments include all kinds of rattles, drums, xylophones, and cymbals. Early percussion instruments were made out of natural materials, such as

Flamenco music is often intense and emotional.

gourds filled with seeds to shake. Animal skins stretched over wooden cylinders created basic drums to beat. The West Indian steel drum was originally designed with natural materials. It is made from used oil drums fitted with a curved metal lid. South American maracas, Spanish castanets, and Asian gongs are all percussion instruments enjoyed by people in many parts of the world.

All of these instruments have evolved further, first with electronics and then with computer programming. In addition to instruments such as the electric guitar and the synthesizer, we also have basic computer programs for making—or composing—music. These offer lots of different sounds. These sounds include new and old instruments and rhythms from around the world. The composer can experiment and create new music with the sounds provided.

Learning & Innovation Skills

Making instruments is a highly skilled craft. Some instruments take many years to learn to make, such as the violin or a **flamenco** guitar. Often families hand down this skill from one generation to the next. Playing instruments, too, requires years of dedication and practice. But the nice thing about music is that you can also make instruments and play them with whatever you have on hand. Try beating on water bottles filled with different amounts of water. Each bottle will create a different pitch. What other basic instruments can you create with materials you have available?

CHAPTER THREE

Freezing Time

For many people, nothing compares to the sound of live music. Live music can be heard at concerts or in local restaurants or cafés. But we hear more recorded music than live music. Recorded music can be heard streaming online, on an MP3 player, or on a CD. We hear music on car radios and in movie theaters when we hear the movie's soundtrack. It's easy to forget that there was a time when recordings did not exist at all. Two innovations in music made it possible for songs to be played again and again, beyond the time of performance.

Have you ever seen music written down? Notes are drawn on a series of lines called a staff. Just like any other language, you have to learn it to understand it. Musical notation was developed in several ancient cultures, such as Greek, Indian, and Chinese. We don't know exactly

why people wanted to develop a way to write music
down. It may be that they loved the songs they made up
and wanted to be able to repeat them exactly. It is also
likely that a lot of early music was created to worship a
deity. People wanted to sing the same songs over and over
in prayer. Somewhere along the line, they figured out that
writing down the notes would allow them to do that.

Devices that attach to instruments and hold sheet
music were a simple, but important invention.
Musicians could march and play instruments
without having to hold music.

Archaeologists have found tablets carved with what they believe to be musical notation in the areas of Mesopotamia, Greece, and Syria. If someone alive today could read this music, we would be able to hear how ancient music sounded. Although ancient people wrote music, the notes didn't look like the kind of music we write today. The form of musical notation used today would not be invented for many years.

The lyre was an important instrument in ancient Greece. It is mentioned in myths and stories about the gods.

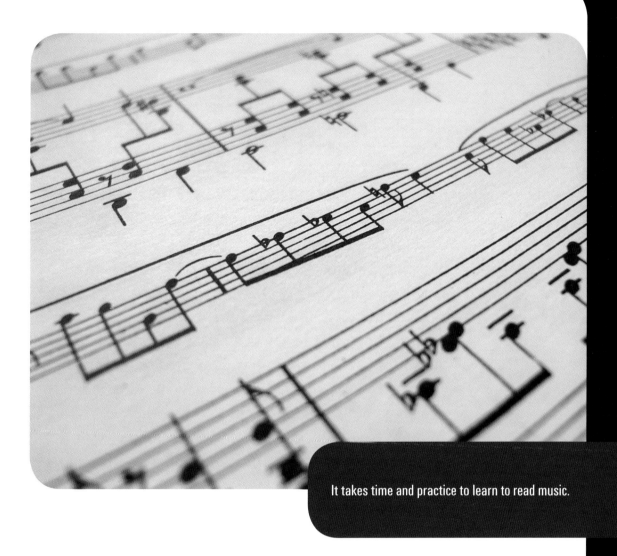

It takes time and practice to learn to read music.

Today's musical notes are shaped like ovals and often have a line on one side. They sit at a particular place on a staff. This determines how the notes are played. This way of writing music has roots in the ancient Greek culture, where philosophers studied and wrote about music along with math, art, and science.

A philosopher named Pythagoras, who lived about 500 BCE, thought music was related to numbers and that rhythm and pitch could **correspond** to numbers. Another man, an Italian monk named Guido of Arezzo, built on these ideas. He combined letters with numbers to make musical notes and added more lines to create a staff. He lived about 1,000 years ago, but his system of writing music survives to this day. If you learn to read music, you can play or sing songs from long ago and far away.

Like notation, the development of recording required experimentation by many people. The first person to successfully record music was the American inventor Thomas Edison. In 1877, Edison invented a machine to record voices and music called the phonograph. Another American, Emil Berliner, developed an **alternative** way to play music on a flat disc that eventually became the record.

Inventors continue to work to improve the quality of recordings. They want to provide the most true-to-life sounds as possible. Today's modern recording studios contain equipment that Edison and other early inventors couldn't even imagine.

Many developments have improved the sound quality, **diversity**, and availability of recorded music. Some of these innovations are so familiar to us now that it is hard to see that they are relative newcomers to music. For example, you might use a Digital Audio Player, or MP3 player, to listen to music. To get music onto this player, it must be transferred from a computer, another fairly new invention. One way to get music files for your computer is from Web sites such as iTunes. These sites allow you to purchase music and download it to your computer. You can also transfer the songs from your compact discs (CDs) to a computer. Then they can be transferred from the computer to an MP3 player.

Digital Audio Players are small but can hold hundreds of songs.

Another way to listen to your favorite music is through a streaming online service such as Napster or Rhapsody. These services allow listeners access to entire catalogs of music for one monthly fee. Napster offers subscribers more than 6 million tracks to chose from. With these services you "rent" the music for as long as you pay the subscription fee. Tracks are also available for purchase.

The Internet makes it easier than ever to find all types of songs and music videos.

Another popular trend in music illustrates the fast pace of recent changes in music technology. In 1981, the first music video television station, MTV, was launched. But today, this once wildly popular innovation is losing steam as more and more people watch videos on popular online sites. These online sites, such as YouTube, feature homemade videos along with professional ones. The Internet makes it possible for young or lesser-known musicians to have their music heard by more people. They create their own videos inexpensively and make them available online. Once again, people who love music have found a way to use new technology to share their music with even more people.

Other inventions have become part of our regular music vocabulary now, such as FM radio, home stereos, and multitrack recording. Can you imagine what the future of music will bring?

Life & Career Skills

Before recording, music was passed down through listening and repetition. Recording allowed musicians to hear new kinds of sounds, which led to much growth and change. For example, jazz musician John Coltrane and the pop band the Beatles were each influenced by Indian music and instruments, such as the sitar. Cellist Yo-Yo Ma has combined classical music with music from Brazil, France, Japan, and other countries. Today, many musicians bridge cultural differences by blending sounds and instruments from different countries to create new forms of music.

CHAPTER FOUR

The Music Industry

Records were the first major method of recording and copying music.

As the music business developed, people were able to hear many new kinds of music. From country and bluegrass to pop and soul, music has **flourished** with the invention of recording. Vinyl records spread the popularity of jazz, blues, and rock bands, leading to the rise of concerts and ticket sales. Technological breakthroughs go hand in hand with new ways to buy and sell products. Recording created big business opportunities.

From the time that Edison and Berliner developed their

Digital technology is quickly replacing CDs in the music world. Some believe that in a few years, CDs will become a thing of the past.

competing systems for playing recorded songs, the music **industry** has proceeded in bursts of technological and marketing innovation. Record companies, such as RCA and Columbia, were started to sell music to the masses. Eventually, records began to be replaced by tape cassettes, and these too were pushed aside with the invention of CDs. Now people can download music from the Internet.

For many years, the music business thrived because people were willing to pay to hear recordings of their favorite musicians. The Internet changed this process. People can now copy CDs onto a computer. Sometimes they share their music files with friends, but this is illegal

21st Century Content

 In 1984, Irish musician Bob Geldof saw a news report about children dying of starvation in Africa and decided to do something about it. Geldof called on friends in the music world to help him record a song called "Do They Know It's Christmas?" The song became an instant hit in the United Kingdom and the United States. Money from sales of the song went to help the people of Africa. Next, Geldof organized a concert called Live Aid. This huge rock concert raised more than $100 million in relief money for Africa. It also helped raise awareness of human rights around the world.

Bono, one of the musicians who took part in Live Aid, traveled to Africa to find out what it was like. He now uses his fame and music to raise awareness and funds for the people of Africa.

and has negatively affected the sales of CDs. It has created legal and other issues that the music industry continues to address.

In response to this, and other changes in the music business, the popular band Radiohead made music history in October 2007 by releasing an album, *In Rainbows*, online. They allowed listeners to choose the price they wanted to pay for the music. It is too early to tell what effect this groundbreaking move will have, but it is clear that the music business is changing once again.

Electronic instruments, the Internet, and specialized computer software have made it possible for musicians to do more themselves. They are able to produce and market their own music. This will likely open the doors to new ways of making, selling, and listening to music.

CHAPTER FIVE

Musical Innovators

Over the years, there have been many innovators who helped music evolve into one of the most universal expressions of art in the world. Here are just a few musicians and composers who changed the face of music forever.

Ludwig van Beethoven

Ludwig van Beethoven is known as one of the greatest and most influential composers in Western classical music. Despite losing

Beethoven's father and grandfather were also musicians.

Learning & Innovation Skills

Imagine that you are at a performance in which Schoenberg introduced his new kind of music. This new music is completely unlike any music you've ever heard before. How would you react? Do you think you would like it or dislike it? Why do you think new kinds of music are difficult for some people to enjoy?

his hearing at a young age, he composed and performed original scores of music. Many people have asked how he knew what a certain note sounded like, if he couldn't hear. Beethoven attached a special rod to the soundboard of the piano. When he played, he would bite down on the rod and feel the vibrations of the notes with his teeth. Even after his death, his music continued to inspire great composers.

Arnold Schoenberg

To understand why this Austrian composer was so revolutionary, we must look at the music that came before him. Music traditionally had harmony. This means that the various notes and chords go together or are held by a structure. Arnold Schoenberg challenged this idea by making music that was atonal—meaning the notes were not related by a key or any other organizing principle. This changed music completely. One of his early students was John Cage, who went on to become one of the most famous American composers of the 20th century.

Some early audiences were upset by Schoenberg's musical style. Schoenberg sometimes felt that people misunderstood his music.

Louis Armstrong

Louis Armstrong, nicknamed Satchmo, is one of the founders of jazz. Before Armstrong, jazz musicians mostly played in small groups. Armstrong began playing his trumpet alone, or solo, during band performances. Soon solos became an important part of jazz music, and he became one of the most popular musicians of all time. He worked hard, playing up to 300 concerts a year all over the world. His many hit recordings are still treasured today.

Part of what made Armstrong special was his ability to improvise, or create variations while he played. Improvisation is a common characteristic of jazz music.

Les Paul

The sounds of contemporary music, particularly rock and roll, are largely attributed to this talented guitarist and inventor. Les Paul is synonymous with the electric guitar he developed and sold to a company called Gibson, which named the guitar after him. A well-known jazz musician and recording artist, Paul developed a way to record himself playing eight unique electric guitar parts on a song. He was the first person known to use multiple tracks, or musical sounds, on one recording—creating the complex musical sound that is so familiar today. His experiments led to multitrack recording and other innovations.

Tony Fadell

Tony Fadell is behind Apple's popular iPod. He imagined a way to connect an MP3 player to an online music store and sell the music through a company. In 2001, he took his idea to the technology company, Apple. He was hired and put in charge of a team that would help to develop what is now known as the iPod. His idea— along with its engineering, development, and marketing at Apple—have changed the way we listen to, buy, sell, and interact with music.

Glossary

adapt (uh-DAPT) to modify or change something to fit a new situation or circumstance

alternative (awl-TUR-nuh-tiv) another choice or option, something that can serve as a substitute

ancient (AYN-shuhnt) very old or in the distant past

archaeologists (ar-kee-OL-uh-jists) people who study objects from the past to understand how people lived

beat (BEET) the pulse of a piece of music, the basic element of rhythm

centuries (SEN-chuh-reez) more than one century; a century is a unit of time equal to 100 years

correspond (kor-uh-SPOND) to be in harmony or agreement, to fit together

didjeridoo (did-JUR-i-doo) a musical instrument of the Aboriginal people of Australia that is made from a long, hollowed branch or stick

diversity (di-VUR-suh-tee) variety, many different kinds

flamenco (fluh-MEN-koh) a kind of music, and a style of dance, from Spain

flourished (FLUR-isht) to have done well, prospered, excelled, or grown

industry (IN-duh-stree) a kind of business or commerce

notes (NOTES) signs to represent single sounds, or it can mean the sounds themselves

percussion (pur-KUHSH-uhn) instruments that make a sound when hit, shaken, or rubbed, like a drum or rattle, or xylophone

pitch (PITCH) the particular sound frequency of a musical instrument, song, or note

rhythm (RITH-uhm) the pattern or timing of sounds in a piece of music

scale (SKALE) a group of musical notes in a defined order

For More Information

BOOKS

Ardley, Neil. *Music*. New York: DK Publishing, Inc., 2004.

Holtz, Martina. *Voggy's ABC's of Music: Basic Music Theory for Kids*. Bonn, Germany: Voggenreiter, 2005.

Johnson, Angela, and Laura Huliska-Beith (illustrator). *Violet's Music*. New York: Dial Books for Young Readers, 2004.

WEB SITES

Howstuffworks—How MP3 Files Work
www.howstuffworks.com/mp3.htm
Learn more about how MP3 files work and how to use them

San Francisco Symphony
www.sfskids.org/templates/splash.asp
Visit this site to find out more about classical music and the symphony orchestra

Index

About the Author

Annie Buckley is a writer, artist, and children's book author. She lives and works in Los Angeles. She has written books about photography, movies, yoga, and creative writing, as well as a biography of the musician Yo-Yo Ma. As a child, Annie played the piano. Now she enjoys listening to many kinds of music such as folk, jazz, and electronic. She had fun investigating music's very long history in writing this book.

Music